Thank you Mr. John and Mrs. Ann Boutwell,
for your lasting dedication to natural
resource conservation and education.

www.mascotbooks.com

Tiny Timber Crew: Travis Visits a Tree Farm

For more information, please contact:
Mascot Kids, an imprint of Amplify Publishing Group
620 Herndon Parkway, Suite 320
Herndon, VA 20170
info@mascotbooks.com

Library of Congress Control Number: 2022911774

CPSIA Code: PRT0722A

ISBN-13: 978-1-63755-239-1

Printed in the United States

Tiny Timber Crew:

Travis VISITS A Tree Farm

Stephanie Fuller

ILLUSTRATED BY
Agus Prajogo and Yohanes Bastian

Travis's class was going to take a trip.
He was so eager to get his
permission slip!

When the exciting day came, the
students—arm in arm—
visited a wonderful place: a great big
tree farm!

Tree farms are home to all kinds of trees.
With a tree farmer's help, there's so much
they can be.

Tree farmers care for their tall crop,
from their roots at the bottom
all the way to their bright green tops.

A group of trees is called a stand.
They live together on a piece of land.

They are all the same in age, size, and height.
Look at them now, their futures are so bright!

Travis was in awe seeing a stand of trees,
whose job was to be harvested and turned into products
for you and me.

Trees make a lot of things you find in the store:
pencils and paper and rulers and more.

Tree farmers have many plans for their trees.
They take care of the animals, land, rivers, and streams.

The stand of trees over there was grown to be a wildlife habitat.
The deer and turkeys and snakes are so excited about that!

Trees give shelter and food to creatures all around.
That's why it's important they're kept safe and sound.

Trees keep streams and rivers healthy and clean.
They're a filter for rainwater and keep shorelines pristine.

Travis and his classmates got to play in a creek.
The water was cold and clear on their feet.

Travis looked all around for fossils galore.
He found one that looked like a snail—
what a score!

To manage a forest is of great concern.
Every so often, it needs a prescribed burn.

Fire, when used right, can be something good.
It clears out some space for fresh, green wood!

It breaks down the grasses and leaves that act as fuel.
It can stop wildfires from spreading—that's pretty cool!

Thinning helps growth by removing competition.
Growing strong, healthy trees is a tree farmer's greatest mission.

Travis was amazed by the tree farm—
so grand and so vast!
The forests are a gift to the future all the
way from the past.

This land is taken care of for a very special goal:
to pass down for generations as the trees grow old.

As Travis left the tree farm, a great big sign he saw.
This green and white diamond shape left him in awe.

The metal sign on the fence, displayed for all to see,
was a promise that this forest would be taken care
of for you and for me.

About the Author

Stephanie Fuller works for the Forest Workforce Training Institute (Forestry Works). Since she grew up rooted in a logging family, it is no surprise that her passion led her to a career in forestry. Stephanie's goal for writing The Tiny Timber Crew series is to educate children about sustainable forestry practices and the people whose job it is to take care of our forests.

ForestryWorks™ is the jobs promotion initiative of the Forest Workforce Training Institute. The mission of ForestryWorks™ is to create a pipeline of workers for the forest industry through education, career promotion, and training. This pipeline will create a sustainable source of forest professionals for generations to come.

Visit forestryworks.com to learn more about jobs in the forest industry.

Visit treefarmsystem.org to learn more about forest stewardship.

The American Tree Farm System® is a network of 70,000 family forest owners sustainably managing 18 million acres of forestland. For over 75 years, ATFS has enhanced the quality of America's woodlands by giving forest owners the tools they need to keep their forests healthy and productive. The American Tree Farm System® is a program of the American Forest Foundation.